I0813457

YOUR LIFE IS A HERO'S JOURNEY!

ALSO BY MISHA MAYNERICK BLAISE

Breathe Deep: An Illustrated Guide to the Transformative Power of Breathing

Crazy for Birds

My Wondrous Cloud Odyssey

This Book Is Made of Clouds

This Phenomenal Life: The Amazing Ways We Are Connected with Our Universe

This Is Texas, Y'all!: The Lone Star State from A to Z

You Are a Cosmic Tree: Baha'i-Inspired Art & Reflections on the Life of the Soul

YOUR LIFE IS A HERO'S JOURNEY!

AN ILLUSTRATED GUIDE TO FACING LIFE'S CHALLENGES

Misha Maynerick Blaise

Andrews McMeel
PUBLISHING®

The authorised representative in the EEA is Simon and Schuster Netherlands BV, Herculesplein 96 3584 AA Utrecht, Netherlands. (info@simonandschuster.nl)

Andrews McMeel Publishing
a division of Andrews McMeel Universal
1130 Walnut Street, Kansas City, Missouri 64106

www.andrewsmcmeel.com

26 27 28 29 30 RLP 10 9 8 7 6 5 4 3 2 1

ISBN: 979-8-8816-0504-9

Library of Congress Control Number: 2025940808

Editor: Danys Mares
Art Director: Holly Swayne
Production Editor: Kelsey Rolofson
Production Manager: Tamara Haus

GET READY

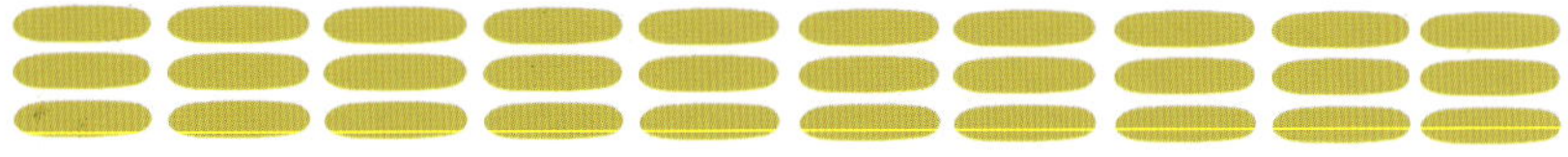

NOTE to the READER:

There are many different versions of the hero's and heroine's journeys. According to psychologist Carl Jung, the hero's journey symbolizes an individual's path to discovering their true self, a process he called "individuation." The stages of the hero's journey reflect phases of psychological growth and transformation. The version I present in this book is an expression of my own personal experience, which blends some elements of both the traditional hero's and heroine's journey and is also just my own thing.

"The journey of the hero is about the
courage to seek the depths;
the image of creative rebirth; the
eternal cycle of change within us;
the uncanny discovery that the
seeker is the mystery which
the seeker seeks to know."

— **JOSEPH CAMPBELL**, *The Hero's Journey: Joseph Campbell and His Life and Work*

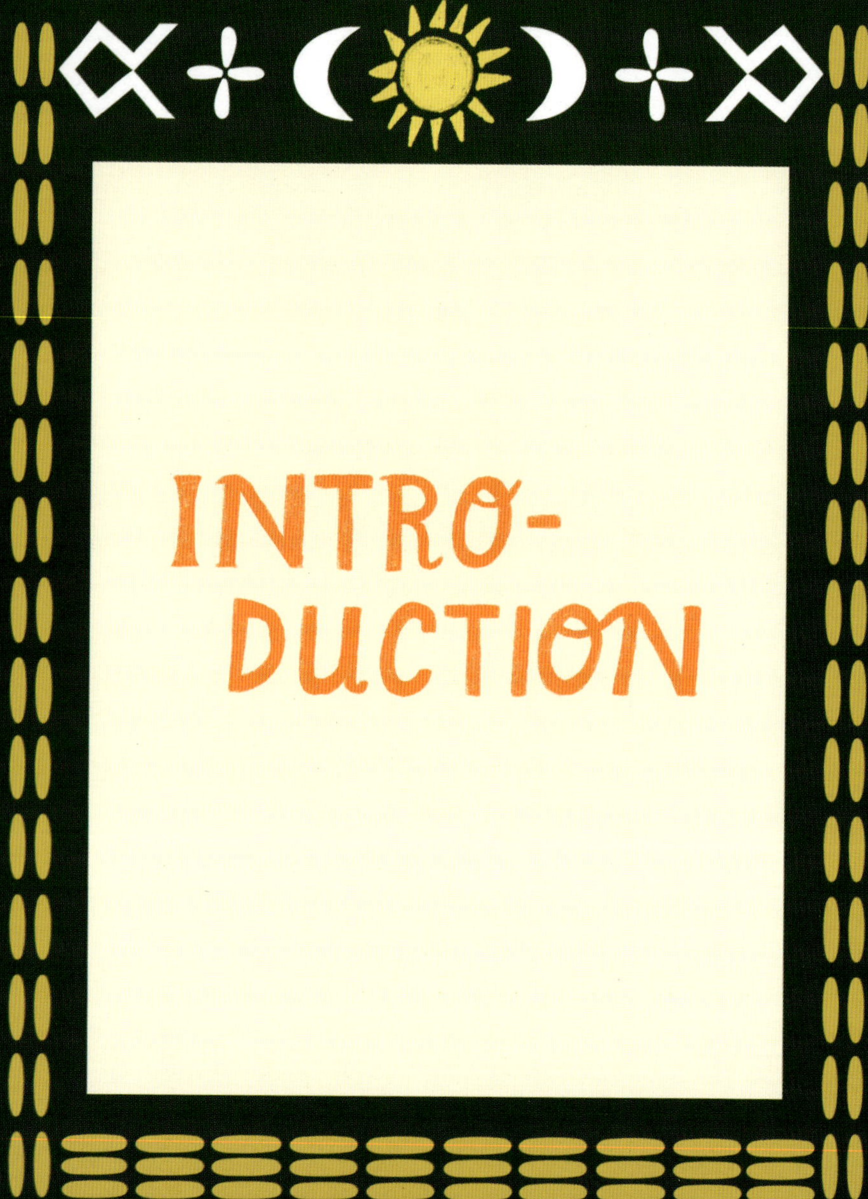

INTRO-DUCTION

It's REALLY HAPPENING.

Your whole life has brought you to this point.

Things have come to pass. Words have been said. Family legacies have unfolded. And now, there is a problem at hand. Daily life is unsettled, not normal. The atoms in the air around you are vibrating with a sense of portent. Life cannot continue on this way; you must do something.

You are being summoned to
A HERO'S JOURNEY!

OH HECK YES!

This is a guide to your coming adventure. It traces the main archetypal themes found in literature and media worldwide.

But don't worry, your own journey will be unique and special. Even though this kind of territory has been traversed by countless people across every culture since the dawn of humanity, what you are going through is different, distinct to your highly personal life circumstances. In other words, even though you're dealing with the extremely common human experience of confronting a massive challenge, no one else is facing your difficulty in all its specifics.

There is no internet search that's going to solve things,
no self-help book that's going to immediately heal your wounds.
There is just a rite of passage staring you in the face,
waiting for you to take the first step.

I WAS BORN FOR THIS!
LET'S GO!

HEADS UP!

YOU ARE GOING TO TRAVEL THROUGH A HELLISH UNDERWORLD.

DON'T WORRY!

THAT TERRIFYING VOID IS PRETTY MUCH JUST THE DEPTHS of your OWN PSYCHE!

The hero's journey relates to developing inner qualities and becoming your true self. Life's path is unpredictable and can't be reduced to a predetermined, fixed scheme.

But some challenges demand extraordinary courage, transforming you along the way. This is the essence of the hero's journey.

STEP 1

THE ORDINARY WORLD

IT'S JUST REGULAR LIFE,
NOTHING TO SEE HERE!

Every journey must begin somewhere, and this one begins in a realm of routine and familiarity known as the ordinary world. It's just life! Your overall worldview is taken for granted, things are the way they are, and there's not much to be done about it (or so you think). No judgment, but you may be just a little overly preoccupied with the trivialities of the world. Or maybe you're caught in old habits and ingrained beliefs, rarely pausing to reflect on why you see things the way you do.

In the far corner of your vision, something appears: a tiny shimmering spark of discontent. It's small enough to ignore, and you may have already ignored it for many years by now. But soon enough, it will ignite a fire.

A flame can be a source of light that gives you vision, a source of heat that provides comfort, or a source of destruction that burns everything down.

The little spark catches your eye again. It's growing more insistent, shape-shifting into a larger form that now dominates your vision. You can no longer deny it; something is about to happen.

STEP 2

THE CALL *to* ADVENTURE

THE CALL TO EMBARK ON THE JOURNEY IS TRIGGERED BY EITHER AN EXTERNAL EVENT OR AN INTERNAL YEARNING.

THERE IS A PROBLEM.

Something is wrong, and you are going to have to deal with it. Maybe never in a million years would you want to deal with this thing, but too bad! That's life, baby!

YOU ARE FEELING OFF-BALANCE
AND YOU DON'T LIKE IT.

Maybe you thought you were on a good path,
but you realize it's not working out.

The universe has stirred things up in a way
that demands your attention.
I'M HERE.
THIS IS the CALL to
ADVENTURE!
But the call is not going to give you a feeling of
joyful expectation; it's going to just feel like trash.

THE ISSUE HAS GROWN TOO BIG AND LOUD TO BE SUPPRESSED; IT MUST BE DEALT WITH.

What's more, no one else can deal with it but you.

Your absolute frustration with the situation has become a compelling force pushing you forward.

STEP 3

REFUSAL of the CALL

THE HERO HESITATES OR RESISTS THE CALL TO ADVENTURE BECAUSE THE RISKS SEEM TOO GREAT.

NOW IS THE TIME TO RUN AWAY AND HIDE!

You're not trying to cause any problems! You were just minding your own business, and a bunch of chaos dropped into your lap for no reason.

Obviously, if you answer the call to adventure, you are taking a big risk.

THINGS THAT MAY HOLD YOU BACK:

Unfortunately, only you can handle this challenge.
If you run away, the journey will be unfulfilled, and this will unleash a whole other kind of hell.

You will FEED YOUR FEAR,
which will grow BIGGER AND
MORE CREATIVE in its METHODS
OF HAUNTING you.

You must rise up and take responsibility for your life.

It's NOW TIME to EMBRACE the ENERGY of THE HERO!
MY TIME IS NOW!

STEP 4

RECEIVE A CONFIRMATION

A MENTOR OF SOME KIND PREPARES THE HERO FOR THE JOURNEY AHEAD.

AN UNEXPECTED

A connection with a friend or mentor, a random book that falls into your hands, a meeting with a support group, or some other life event resonates in a way that is deeply reassuring.

At the SUPPORt GROUP:

A MYSTICAL
GUIDE of SOME
SORt GIVES you
WINGS.

This feeling of confirmation can show up at other points in the journey, too. It's a feature of the cosmic design that once you direct your energies toward the higher good, a supernatural force will swoop in to give you the boost of support that you need.

Acknowledge the presence of this guide when you recognize it.
Give thanks and continue on your way.

STEP 5

CROSSING *the* THRESHOLD

THE HERO LEAVES BEHIND THE FAMILIAR AND ENTERS AN UNKNOWN OR EXTRAORDINARY WORLD.

The moment has arrived to enter the great unknown. You are crossing the threshold—which basically means you are leaving your comfort zone, facing uncertainty, and seeking a new perspective on life.

Let's face the facts: Your initial efforts might be a total mess. Things are already in disarray, and the whole problem is that you don't have answers. Since you don't yet know how to best deal with the situation, you may act out and repeat old, dysfunctional patterns.

You may live a double life for a while as you try to expand into a new way of being.

At work:

Alone at home:

The CHALLENGES ARE coming At you FULL FORCE IN THIS PHASE.

It may be counterintuitive, but try to go toward the difficult situations, even if you take baby steps.

(Like the size of a MICROSCOPIC water bear)

Just like muscles grow stronger with exercise, you will gain emotional and psychological strength when you embrace discomfort as an opportunity for growth rather than something to be feared.

This phase may not be pleasurable, but at least things are changing (you hope!).

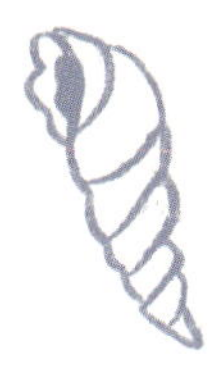
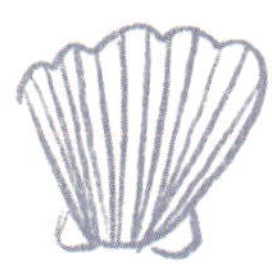

"WHETHER WE ARE CONSCIOUSLY AWARE OF IT OR NOT, WE ARE ALL REPEATEDLY FACED WITH CHANCES to BECOME INITIATED INTO OUR LIFE'S SECRET PURPOSE."

—LISA MARCHIANO

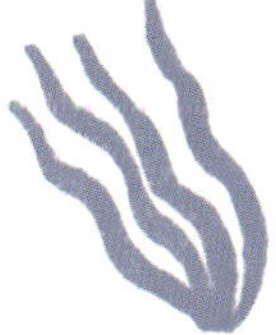

Step 6

TESTS, ALLIES, and ENEMIES

THIS STAGE REVEALS THE HERO'S STRENGTHS AND WEAKNESSES.

Study, take action, and reflect. Your active engagement with your issues stirs up energy that attracts different forces.

THERE WILL BE THOSE WHO SUPPORT YOU:

These allies can help you realize virtues you didn't know you had, and it's deeply relieving to receive encouragement when you're going through a difficult time. The ability to grow stronger through adversity is often linked to having social support. The strength of these relationships highlights feelings of empathy, collaboration, and mutual respect.

THERE WILL ALSO BE THOSE WHO OPPOSE YOU:

These adversaries stir up your unresolved wounds, weaknesses, or past mistakes. This is super annoying and may trigger feelings of anger, pride, or defensiveness. In some cases, you may be struggling against an antagonistic person or situation that is making your life miserable. Recognizing these malevolent forces brings clarity to your mission and strengthens your resolve.

While personal or ideological enemies can serve as important catalysts for growth, it's crucial to avoid the trap of dividing the world into simplistic "us" and "them" categories. In this stage, the true enemies are the influences that lead you to view people as political abstractions rather than as complex, real human beings. (Even though you may need space from some of those real human beings.)

Your tests, allies, and enemies are like mirrors that reveal your strengths and weaknesses. This self-insight not only strengthens your character but also prepares you for the greater obstacles ahead.

The adversity you are facing is pushing you to develop new skills and strategies. But even though you are building up confidence, you are about to be met with a challenge that feels too big to overcome.

"THE CAVE you FEAR to ENTER HOLDS the TREASURE you SEEK."

Attributed to JOSEPH CAMPBELL

STEP 7

ENTER THE VOID

THE HERO FACES A PROFOUND FEAR, A LIFE-OR-DEATH MOMENT, OR A DEEP INNER CRISIS.

By rejecting the way things were, you have caused a great disruption. You have torn the fabric of the known cosmic order. Your previous map of reality no longer aligns with the world you're entering. Things have been thrown into chaos.

You can't just solve the problems. You need a whole new framework to understand life, but you don't have it yet.

This is the
DARK
NIGHT
of the
SOUL.

Confusion and hopelessness rule in this abyss. You wrestle with the nature of reality, the existence of evil, and the fact of suffering. What once made sense is now turned upside down. You feel a deep vulnerability as you confront unresolved traumas or repressed emotions. The turbulence of your inner world feels like too much to handle, and you feel disconnected from your sense of purpose.

While stumbling through the shadowy underground labyrinth of your psyche, you may happen upon inner shame, fears, and insecurities. This sends you even deeper into despair.
WHAT ARE you GUYS DOING IN HERE?
SHAME
FEARS
INSECURITIES

This is the precise moment when you will lift yourself up from the gutter long enough to browse social media and see that the most terrible, obnoxious guy you know is doing just fine. Excellent, even. He's at the peak of his life and career! You will even notice a few of your own friends amongst his admirers.

This phase involves regret and longing:

This is the ultimate face-off between you and your source.

You feel raw and exposed as the anchors to your old life—like your identity, purpose, and even hope—are stripped away. Even your spiritual guides cannot bring their light into this dark and forsaken place.

What's even more devastating is that your usual distractions no longer work; things that once brought comfort now feel hollow. This is a place of pure chaos and isolation, an underworld that seems inescapable.

Note: If you give up in this abyss, you are doomed to repeat your lessons. Anguish and malaise will continue. But don't worry, there will be many more opportunities to confront this harrowing inferno!

STEP 8

ALL IS LOST

THIS IS A MOMENT OF PROFOUND DESPAIR WHEN THE HERO FACES THEIR DARKEST HOUR.

That's it. Your skill set has failed you. There is no happy ending, no ultimate solution. It was all for nothing. This stage marks the hero's collapse, an emotional low point when all seems hopeless. Naked and shivering before the unknowable essence that rules the universe, there's nothing left to do but admit you are a mere mortal who will never understand or be able to control everything.

LIFE IS
A MESS
AND SO
ARE YOU!

"IN ALL CHAOS
THERE IS A COSMOS,
IN ALL DISORDER
A SECRET ORDER..."

—CARL JUNG

This phase is a coming to terms with the deep mystery of suffering that is built into the divine plan. There is no avoiding it, no way to make ultimate sense of it. Maybe it all could have gone differently, but it didn't. There is no reconciliation; several elements of your life exist in dramatic tension with one another, and it might be like that forever.

The old ways are lost, but in a sense, that's a good thing. Only now can you undergo true change. You understand that in life, struggle is not a sign of failure but a pathway to deeper wisdom and strength. This can be a turning point, an opportunity to rebuild and reimagine your path forward!

If good fortune shines upon you, a guide will now appear to provide a much-needed swig of soul-inspiration juice to propel you onward once more. Otherwise, you must go it alone. Faced with self-doubt, it's time to decide whether to give up or rise again!

KEEP GOING!

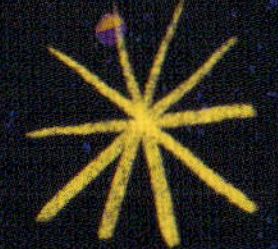

STEP 9

The ORDEAL

THE HERO IS PUSHED TO THE LIMIT!

In this moment of giving up your smallest self and putting your faith in something higher, you summon a deep courage from within to survive. You are humbled to your core, aware that your entire life is dependent on a greater, more transcendent power.

YOU SEND A SIGNAL OUT TO the UNIVERSE:

With no other choice left, you tap into a wellspring of inner resources you didn't even know you had. Emboldened by how absolutely sick and tired you are of this seemingly endless dumpster fire, you take action!

With great discernment, you figure out which dragons need to be slain and which ones need embracing.

Your journey forces you to confront your fears, wounds, inner contradictions, and the limitations of your current approach to life. But a shift is happening. Although you may still feel broken, you are learning to have more compassion for your broken self. The pain doesn't magically disappear, but your relationship with it is changing.

"IF WE ARE to FIND
OUR OWN INNER TRUTH,
WE HAVE to GO INTO OUR
DARKNESS ALONE and STAY with
OUR OWN INNER PROCESS
UNTIL WE FIND OUR OWN
HEALING ARCHETYPAL PATTERN."

—MARION WOODMAN

STEP 10

THE REWARD

HAVING CONFRONTED THEIR SHADOWS, FEARS, AND LIMITATIONS, THE HERO HAS GAINED A DEEPER UNDERSTANDING OF THEIR TRUE SELF.

Suddenly you emerge from the dense fog of your struggles
into a place of clarity.

A renewal of hope blossoms forth.
You feel a deepened sense of assurance.

Doubts, fears, and illusions held by the old self are outgrown and replaced with a fresh perspective.

You may feel stronger, wiser, or more connected to your purpose, even if you don't yet fully understand the crisis you just navigated. You don't forget the pain, but you can embrace its gift.

Despite the incredible progress that's been made, you may be surprised to find that you have not completely transcended the disarray of life. Even as you meet challenges with increased skill, you may notice that you are, in fact, still human. But with increased emotional maturity, it's easier for you to embrace your imperfections.

The overarching fear of failure that may have plagued you in earlier times has subsided. You strive for excellence, unburdened by unrealistic standards imposed by some tyrannical inner perfectionist or rigid social customs. You've gained a deeper sense of self-awareness and authenticity.

YOU CAN EXPRESS YOUR UNIQUE SELF IN AN IMPERFECT WORLD...

...AT PEACE with your FLAWS AND your STRENGTHS.

At this moment, you are confidently equipped with an arsenal of mantras to help you resist perfectionism:

LIFE IS A BIG MESS!

I WILL INEVITABLY EXPERIENCE PAIN AND SUFFERING.

...THEN COMES TOGETHER...

GREAT!

...THEN FALLS APART AGAIN.

OH WELL!

I AM IMPERFECT.

I WILL NEVER UNDERSTAND EVERYTHING.

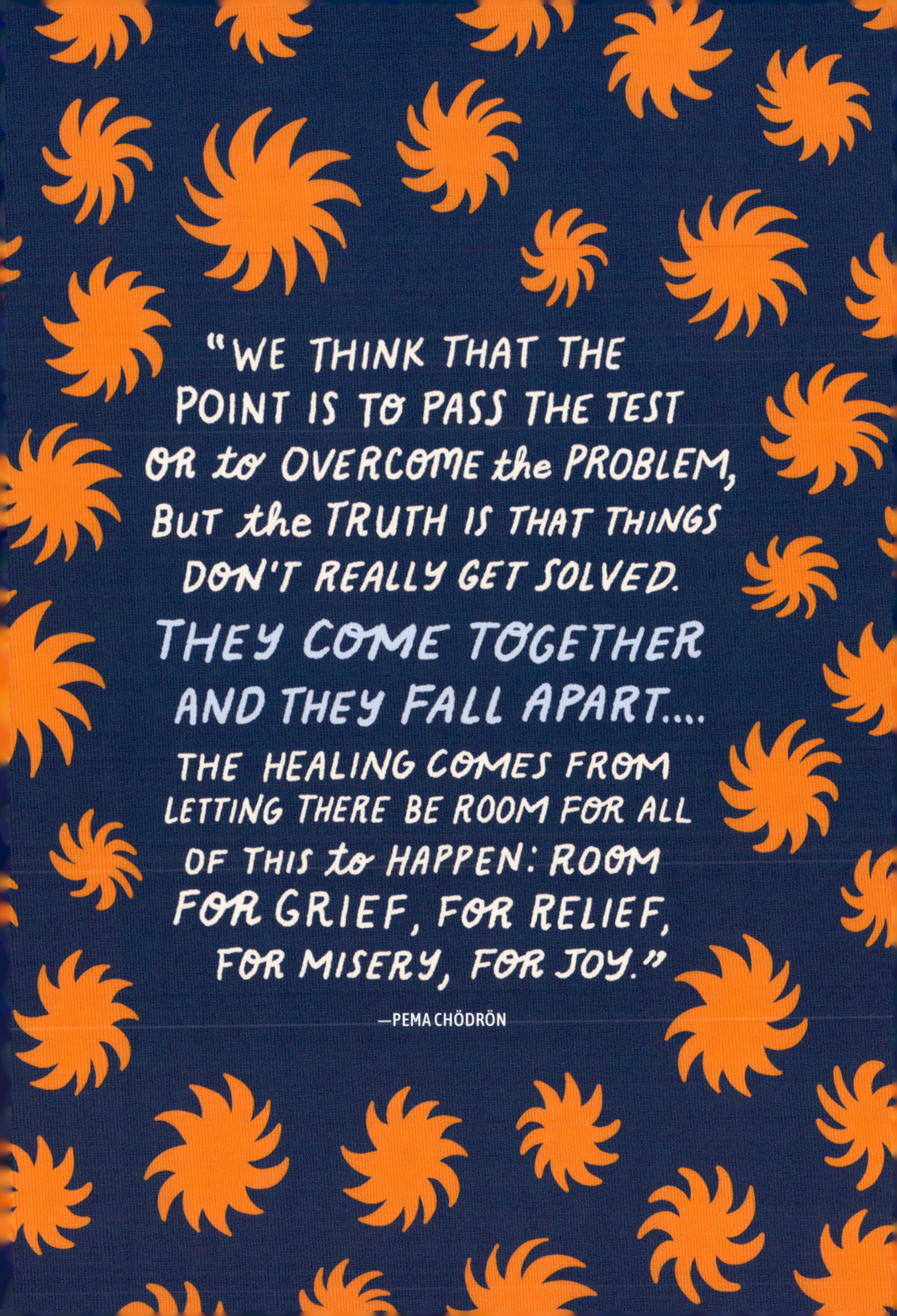
"WE THINK THAT THE
POINT IS TO PASS THE TEST
OR to OVERCOME the PROBLEM,
BUT the TRUTH IS THAT THINGS
DON'T REALLY GET SOLVED.
THEY COME TOGETHER
AND THEY FALL APART....
THE HEALING COMES FROM
LETTING THERE BE ROOM FOR ALL
OF THIS to HAPPEN: ROOM
FOR GRIEF, FOR RELIEF,
FOR MISERY, FOR JOY."
—PEMA CHÖDRÖN

It's now possible to embrace the paradox that imperfection and wholeness can, and must, coexist. You will never escape the demands of life, but fear of failure no longer holds you back from living more fully.

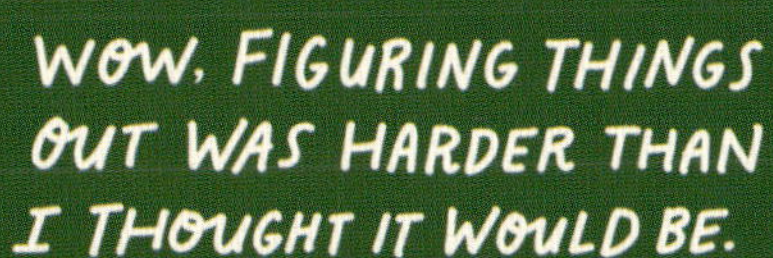

STEP 11

THE ROAD BACK

THE HERO RETURNS TO
THE ORDINARY WORLD
BUT FACES A FINAL TEST.

It's time to reenter ordinary life.

As a fun little cosmic joke, you almost immediately face a situation that tests your new way of being.

This test is perfectly designed for your personality, as if the universe knows just the thing to send you back into chaos. It is now time to truly embody the changes you've undergone.

Previously, this situation might have launched you into absolute panic or feelings of life-or-death desperation. The old you would have been sent spiraling off into a dysfunctional vortex.

But now, you have the wherewithal to see the challenge for what it is and pause before you act. Your fear might still be there as a constant companion, but it no longer controls you.

You feel a calm confidence (even if it's still a little shaky) knowing that you have improved skills and insights to handle the situation.

Driven by a renewed sense of purpose and supported by your guides, you engage the challenge with a clear vision. Overcoming adversity has helped you develop grit, perseverance, and confidence to handle life's inevitable difficulties. You turn what was once a formidable obstacle into a manageable task that validates your journey of transformation!

STEP 12

RETURN WITH AN ELIXIR

THE HERO BRINGS KNOWLEDGE, WISDOM, OR A GIFT TO SHARE WITH THEIR COMMUNITY.

A change has occurred. You aren't the same person you were when you set out.

THE VOYAGE INTO THE VOID
HAS OPENED A DEEPER DIMENSION
OF YOUR SOUL.

You now have a richer understanding of yourself and the world.
You see reality with new eyes.

You have discovered the true reasons for your journey:

I USE MY DIFFICULTIES TO DEVELOP EMPATHY AND CONNECT WITH OTHERS.
I CAN EMBRACE THE ONGOING CYCLE OF TRIALS, GROWTH, AND TRANSFORMATION.
I HAVE DISCOVERED MORE ABOUT MY TRUE SELF!

YOUR LIFE WILL NEVER BE THE SAME.

Now you must return to the ordinary world and use the gifts you have gained to benefit others. Your new elixir can help resolve the problems that initially spurred your departure, bringing peace, inspiration, restoration, or healing.

The impact of your journey extends beyond your personal story, affecting the larger narrative of society. With your increased wisdom, you actively seek ways to contribute to the well-being of your community and find like-minded people to collaborate with.

You realize your twofold moral purpose: to attend to your own spiritual growth and to contribute to the advancement of society. Insight finds expression in social involvement and service. Personal success was never the ultimate goal; the true fulfillment of your mission lies in your ability to help uplift others. You find ways to support other budding heroes along their journeys!

This stage highlights the cyclical nature of the journey, where the end also marks a new beginning. The path is not a straight line; it is a spiral. You may revisit old wounds, but with your expanded vision, you have the opportunity to heal them at a deeper level. You have increased your skill set to confront adversity rather than avoid it.

THE COSMIC OUROBOROS

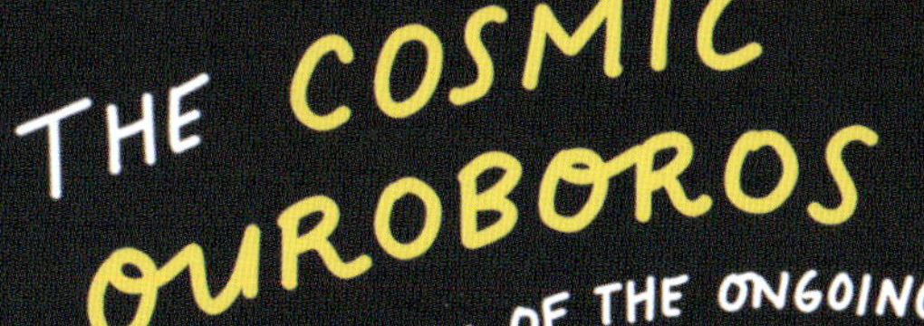

REMINDS you OF THE ONGOING CYCLES OF LIFE and DEATH AND THE PARADOX of CREATION.

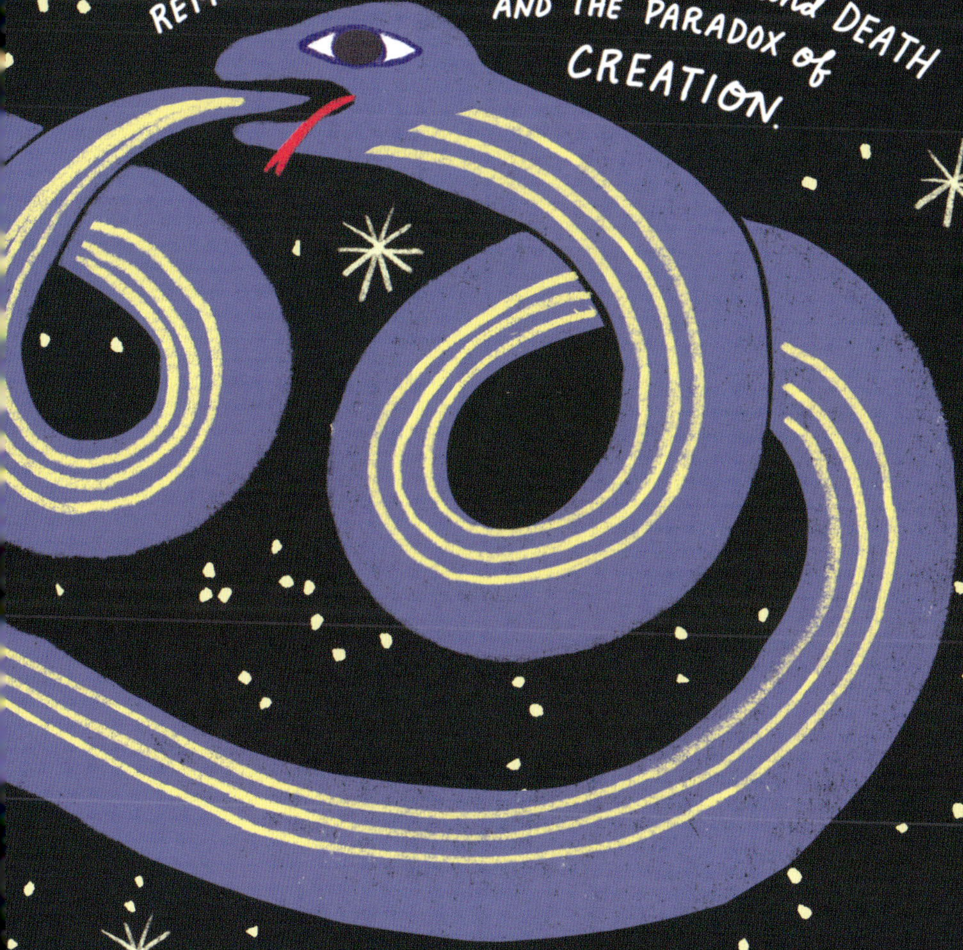

Life is going to keep coming at you, but you are ready to face challenges and thrive in an unpredictable world.

IT'S NOW TIME FOR
ANOTHER JOURNEY.

AND MORE
CUDDLES!

NO
THANK
YOU.

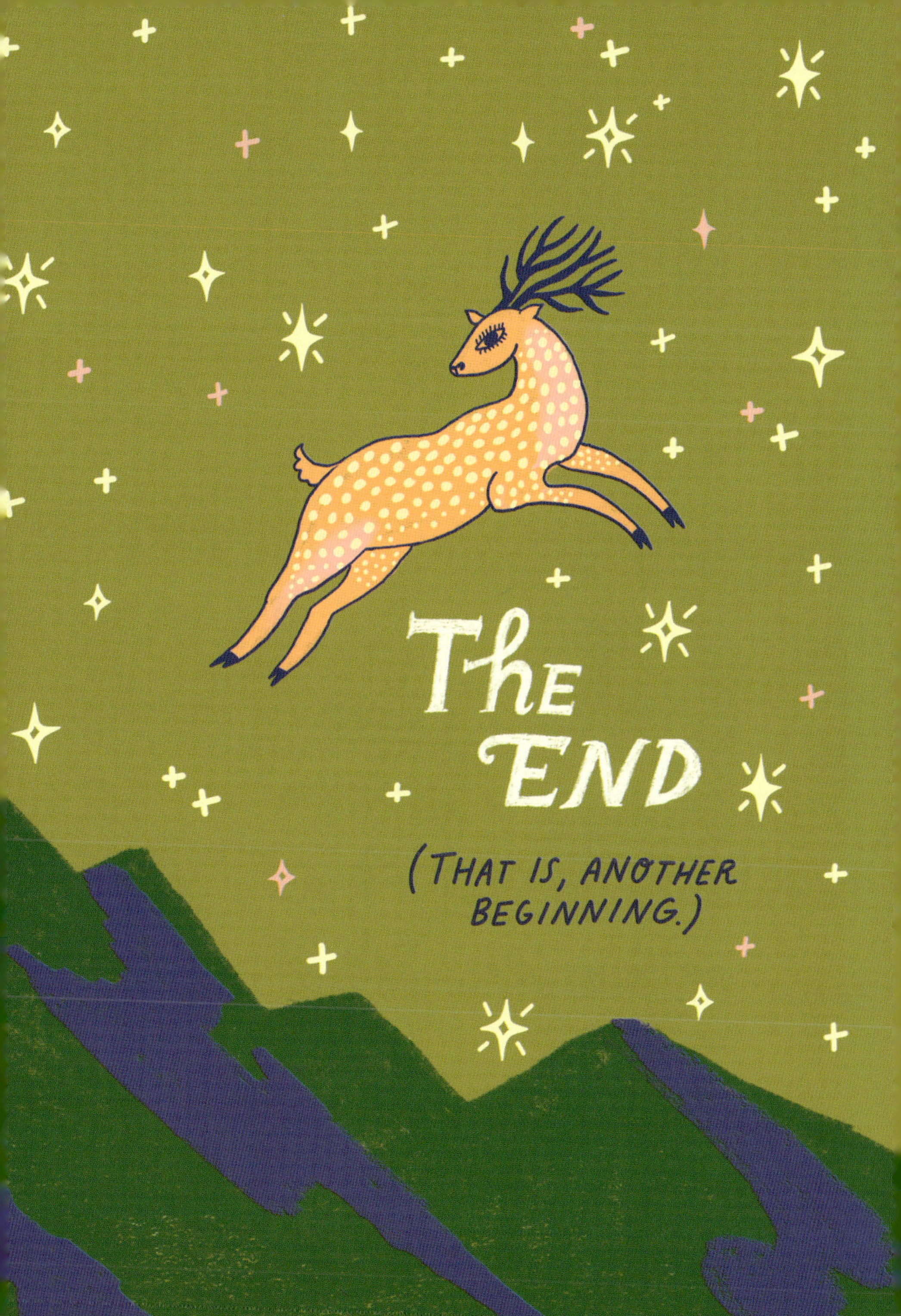
The END
(THAT IS, ANOTHER BEGINNING.)

WITHIN the HEART of EVERY
CHALLENGE LIES the CHANCE
to DISCOVER the
STRENGTH
you NEVER
KNEW you
HAD.

FINAL THOUGHTS

While writing this book, I was surprised to find that there has been some psychological research about how the narrative of the hero's journey can have a positive impact on mental health. As humans, we seek meaning through the stories we tell. Using the framework of the hero's journey, people can reframe what they've been through in life as part of a coherent growth process.

This is the power of the hero's journey as a narrative. It's a way to reevaluate your life and think of difficult situations as part of a larger epic story. Our daily lives can feel mundane, and our problems can feel miserable, but by seeing your story through the lens of the hero's journey, you can find its greater meaning. Taking a bird's-eye view, even across generations, allows you to see how far you've come. You can see your life as a story and your experiences as metaphors for deeper psychospiritual processes.

If you're still in the throes of difficulty, the hero's narrative empowers your continued efforts and assures you that it will all lead somewhere, somehow. Suffering may lead to greater insight, but pain hurts—and naturally, we seek to avoid it. We are afraid it will break us. Being thrown into the underworld is a common theme in classic fairy tales. No one willingly chooses to go there, yet at some point, we all find ourselves in that dark place. True transformation, however, is only possible through facing life's most difficult challenges. Grappling with the hidden or unrealized aspects of the self as part of the hero's journey can increase resilience, improve well-being, and foster inner strength.

What we do with our pain influences how we experience life. Many spiritual traditions speak of the transformative power of consciously facing challenges. The first noble truth in Buddhism is that suffering is an inevitable part of the human experience, not a punishment or a flaw. This understanding helps us face suffering honestly without trying to deny or avoid it. Saint John of the Cross, a Christian mystic, spoke of the dark night of the soul, a feeling of deep alienation from God and one's purpose. This harrowing time can be seen as a rite of passage necessary for refinement and renewal. The Bahá'í Faith teaches that confronting difficulties is an essential part of spiritual growth that can help us build capacity and gain wisdom. The hero's journey speaks to this pattern of descent, transformation, and return that is also part of initiation rites around the world.

When the hero returns with the elixir, their newfound wisdom and insight is thought to radiate outward, positively influencing the greater community. When you've personally experienced the transmutation of suffering into growth, it fundamentally reshapes your belief in the human spirit's capacity to change and become stronger. Knowing that your own evolution has had its ups and downs, you can maintain a steady sense of hope, even as the world faces ongoing cycles of crisis and victory. This realization inspires deep confidence, not only for other individuals who may feel stuck but for humanity as a whole. The emotional maturity and spiritual awareness gained through an individual hero's journey suggests that society, too, has the potential to advance for the better. Upon return, the hero also feels a sense of responsibility to contribute to the greater good. The world's problems are no longer seen as distant or unchangeable but as challenges that require collective effort. The hero collaborates with others to read reality and take constructive action.

While the word "hero" may seem to refer to someone extraordinary, it actually describes an ordinary person like you or me, navigating the unique circumstances life has given each of us. I believe we should take from the narrative whatever serves our own growth, rather than using it as a rigid formula to judge others. I would never want to minimize or dismiss people's personal challenges or claim that everything happens for a reason. Not everyone experiences healing or transformation in the same way or on the same timeline, and I'm not sure everyone finds a "happy ending." I just know that my struggles have helped me better accept what is, and that might be the closest thing there is to resolution. The hero's journey framework should be used with sensitivity in a way that's useful but doesn't minimize your own or others' experiences.

Ultimately, I think the hero's journey is a story about love. It teaches us that love is not just an emotion but a powerful force that can drive us to face the most daunting challenges, heal our deepest wounds, and confront the forces that hold us back. The hero is pushed to the limit and hurled down into the darkest underworld, but through the spark of love, the hero finds the inner resources to go on. The love received from others provides assurance and comfort along the way.

The hero's journey reveals a profound truth: Tests and difficulties can awaken the soul's deepest powers of faith, courage, and creative action. Fortunately (or unfortunately), life will continue to present us with challenges, each one an invitation to step forward and embark on our very own hero's journey, again and again!

QUESTIONS FOR YOUR INNER HERO

1. THE ORDINARY WORLD

What does your "ordinary world" look like right now? Do you sense any glimmer of change appearing at the edge of your vision? Is there anything that feels slightly off, as if something in your life is about to shift or break open?

2. CALL TO ADVENTURE

Can you identify a moment in your life that felt like a "call to adventure"? Did it interest you, scare you, or both? How were you able to move forward?

3. REFUSAL OF THE CALL

When have you hesitated to act during a turning point in your life, and what held you back? What forces, either internal or external, tend to keep you from stepping forward to face your challenges or seize your opportunities?

4. RECEIVE A CONFIRMATION

Who or what has served as a mentor or guide in your life? Who has supported you during a time of uncertainty or transition, and what did you learn from them?

5. CROSSING THE THRESHOLD

What is one moment in your life when you left the familiar behind and stepped into the unknown? What did you risk, and what did you discover?

6. TESTS, ALLIES, AND ENEMIES

Who in your life has helped you uncover strengths or virtues you didn't know you had? Who has set off feelings of anger or defensiveness?

What might those reactions be telling you about yourself? Have you ever misjudged someone as an ally or enemy, only to later discover something unexpected about them, or about yourself?

7. ENTER THE VOID

Have you ever found yourself in a place where your usual beliefs, roles, or coping mechanisms no longer made sense? What's it like when you're caught between who you used to be and who you're becoming but have no clear direction forward?

8. ALL IS LOST

Have you ever had to face a situation that you couldn't fix or control? What did that experience teach you about yourself or the nature of reality? Are there parts of your life that seem permanently unresolved or in tension? How might accepting that tension create space for wisdom or growth?

9. THE ORDEAL

What is one of the hardest moments you've lived through, and what part of you had to be released or transformed in order to make it through?

10. THE REWARD

What insight, strength, or gift have you gained from a difficult experience?

11. THE ROAD BACK

After a period of profound change, how did you reenter ordinary life? What felt different, and what stayed the same?

12. RETURN WITH THE ELIXIR

What wisdom or healing do you now carry that you would like to share with others if the opportunity arises? How can your personal transformation contribute to the well-being of your community or the world?

BIBLIOGRAPHY

Campbell, Joseph. *The Hero's Journey: Joseph Campbell and His Life and Work*. New World Library, 2014.

Chödrön, Pema. *When Things Fall Apart: Heart Advice for Difficult Times*. Shambhala, 1996.

Jung, Carl Gustav. *The Archetypes and the Collective Unconscious*. Vol. 9, part 1, *The Collected Works of C. G. Jung*, edited by Gerhard Adler and R. F. C. Hull. Princeton University Press, 1981.

Marchiano, Lisa. *Motherhood: Facing and Finding Yourself*. Sounds True, 2021.

Rogers, B. A., H. Chicas, J. M. Kelly, et al. "Seeing Your Life Story as a Hero's Journey Increases Meaning in Life." *Journal of Personality and Social Psychology* 125, no. 4 (2023): 752–778. https://doi.org/10.1037/pspa0000341.

Woodman, Marion. *Addiction to Perfection: The Still Unravished Bride*. Inner City Books, 1982.

ABOUT THE AUTHOR

Misha Maynerick Blaise is an author-illustrator known for the fresh and original style of her illustrated gift books. She enjoys exploring themes of interconnectedness, the mysteries of the universe, self-discovery, and the human experience. She lives with her husband and two sons in northwest Arkansas. Visit her at mishablaise.com.